UNDERSTA

The
Presence
of God

Also by Selwyn Hughes in this series

Understanding Guidance
Understanding Communion

(to be published May 1991)

UNDERSTANDING
The Presence of God

by
Selwyn Hughes

CWR, Waverley Abbey House,
Waverley Lane, Farnham, Surrey GU9 8EP

NATIONAL DISTRIBUTORS
Australia: Christian Marketing Pty Ltd., PO Box 154,
North Geelong, Victoria 3215.
Tel: (052) 786100
Canada: Christian Marketing Canada Ltd.,
PO Box 7000, Niagara on the Lake, Ontario LOS 1TO.
Tel: 416 641 0631
Republic of Ireland: Merrion Press Ltd.,
10 D'Olier Street, Dublin.
Tel & Fax: 773316
Malaysia: Salvation Book Centre, (M) Sdn. Bhd.,
23 Jalan SS2/64, 47300 Petaling Jaya, Selangor
New Zealand: CWR (NZ), PO Box 4108,
Mount Maunganui 3030.
Tel: (075) 757412
Singapore: Alby Commercial Enterprises Pte Ltd.,
Garden Hotel, 14 Balmoral Road, Singapore 1025
Southern Africa: CWR (Southern Africa), PO Box 43,
Kenilworth 7745, South Africa.
Tel: (021) 7612560

© CWR 1991
Text originally published 1988, revised and first printed in this format
1991

Typeset by J&L Composition Ltd, Filey, North Yorkshire

Printed in Great Britain by Richard Clay Ltd,
Bungay, Suffolk

ISBN 1–85345–042–1

Contents

INTRODUCTION

"Behold, I stand at the door and knock.
If anyone hears my voice and opens the door,
I will come in ..."
(Revelation 3:20, NKJ)

Christians have the assurance that they are constantly surrounded by the presence of God, and that the Almighty's presence abides with them through thick and thin. For He has said: "I will never leave you nor forsake you" (Heb. 13:5, NKJ). And again: "He keeps his eye upon you as you come and go, and always guards you" (Psalm 121:8, TLB).

Honesty compels us to admit, however, that although Scripture assures us that we are constantly guarded and surrounded by the presence of God, we do not always feel it. There could be many reasons for this, of course, but let it be understood right away that if we do not regularly experience God's presence in our lives, the fault is always in us, never in Him. We ask ourselves therefore: what can we do to practise the presence of God in our lives? In other words, how can we increase, enhance and understand better the sense of God's presence? How can we sharpen our spiritual awareness?

Before we look at some of the ways in which this can be done, we must make the point that no one can practise the presence of God until first they know God. The practice of religious techniques and methods may be helpful to those who know Him, but He can never be known by them alone. How then do we come to know God and experience a personal encounter with Him? It begins when we stop struggling to save ourselves and consent to let Him be our Saviour. If you have never surrendered your life to Christ, then I urge you, do it right now. Start right by getting right with God.

PRAYER

My Father and my God, I see that I cannot know Your presence until first I know You. I surrender my life into Your hands – this very moment. You have me, Lord – and now I have You. I am so thankful. Amen.

Chapter 1

GETTING TO KNOW GOD

*"Come near to God and he will come
near to you."*
(James 4:8, NIV)

Before we can practise the presence of God, we must
first come to know God. Those who are Christians
must bear with me as I press this point, for some
reading these lines will know about God but have
never had a personal encounter with Him. We must
gather up every seeking soul before moving on.

The lost sheep

The answer to the question, "How do I find God?" is
this: you do not have to find Him, you simply have to
let Him find you. If the Bible teaches us anything, it
teaches us that not only does man search for God but
God searches for man. Look at Luke chapter 15:3–7
(NIV):

"Then Jesus told them this parable: 'Suppose one
of you has a hundred sheep and loses one of them.

Does he not leave the ninety-nine in the open country and go after the lost sheep until he finds it? And when he finds it, he joyfully puts it on his shoulders and goes home. Then he calls his friends and neighbours together and says, 'Rejoice with me; I have found my lost sheep.' I tell you that in the same way there is more rejoicing in heaven over one sinner who repents than over ninety-nine righteous persons who do not need to repent."

What is Jesus trying to say in this parable, and the other two parables, the parables of the lost silver and the lost son (Luke chapter 15:8–32)? He is saying that the God of the universe is involved in a persistent and redemptive search for us. How amazing! "In finding God," said Mahatma Gandhi to a missionary, "you must have as much patience as a man who sits by the seaside and undertakes to empty the ocean, lifting up one drop of water with a straw."

The great man was wrong. These parables tell us why as they fling back the curtains and let us see the God of the shepherd-heart who seeks and seeks for the lost sheep until He finds it; the God who sweeps the universe with the broom of His redemptive grace until He finds the coin on which His image is stamped; the God whose love is so powerful that it lays siege to the hearts of those who have run from their Father's house. The thrilling truth is this, you do not have to seek laboriously to find God, you simply have to let Him find you. Accept the gift of Himself and then belong forever to the Giver.

Key of repentance

This must not be understood, however, to mean that God has done everything possible to save us and that our individual salvation is now an automatic thing. God has gone to the utmost lengths to save us, but in order to be saved, we must turn to Him in an act of contrition and repentance and invite Him to take up residence within us. We saw in the introduction that in Revelation chapter 3:20 Jesus says He stands at the door of our lives, asking to come in. In the previous verse, He reveals that the key that unlocks that door is repentance: "Therefore be zealous and repent. Behold, I stand at the door and knock . . ." (Revelation 3:19–20, NKJ).

I have met some people who think that because they have felt God's presence in their lives at one time or another, this is sufficient evidence to believe that they are favoured by the Almighty and have no need to invite Him into their hearts. They say things like this: "I know God is with me because He protected me from a serious accident." Or, "I felt His presence in an awesome way at the birth of my child." Or again, "I felt God's presence surround me during an operation."

I have no doubt that many people sense God's presence around them, but they can never sense God's presence within them until they invite Him to come in. He loves every one of His creation, but He loves them too much to gate-crash the personality. He comes in only as we give our consent. "No one is constitutionally incapable of finding God," says Billy Graham. If we do not find Him, then the problem is not in our constitution but in our consent. When, by an act of the will, you decide to let God in, then believe me, nothing in earth or heaven can keep Him out.

Now that we are clear about the fact that we cannot practise the presence of God until He resides within us, we are ready to begin looking at some of the things we can do to help us become more conscious and more aware of His indwelling presence.

Chapter 2

GOOD MORNING, LORD

"When I awake, I am still with you."
(Psalm 139:18, NIV)

Our first thought upon waking ought to be of the Lord. A friend of mine says that this suggestion, given to him in the early days of his Christian experience, has been the means of sharpening the sense of God's presence in his life more than almost any other single thing. Listen to how an unknown poet put it:

"Every morning lean thine arm awhile
Upon the window sill of heaven
And gaze upon thy God;
Then with the vision in thy heart
Turn strong to meet the day."

"Turn strong to meet the day." What an optimistic thought! And why not? Anyone who looks into the face of God during the waking moments is fortified to look into the face of anything the day may bring.

Someone has said there are two kinds of Christians; those who wake up in the morning, look around the room and say rather gloomily: "Oh, Lord, another day," and those who wake up, look into their heavenly Father's face and say brightly: "Oh, Lord, another day!" Which kind, I wonder, are you?

Influential thinking

Those who study the effect of thought upon the personality tell us that our last thought at night and our first thought in the morning are greatly influential in determining the quality of our sleep and our attitudes toward life. We shall talk about the importance of the last thought at night a little later on, but for the moment, we will continue to consider the importance of focusing your waking thoughts on God. How will this help? It gives a divine perspective to the day.

If your day begins with God, it is more likely to continue and end with Him. How we start determines to a great degree the way we go on and the way we finish. Some Christians say that it helps to sharpen their awareness of the fact that God is with them if they turn to Him as soon as they are awake and say, "Good morning, Lord." Sentimental? Some might think so, but if there is one thing I have learned in my Christian experience, it is the fact that what suits one may not suit another.

Whatever method you use to focus your thoughts on God in the first few moments after you awake is not important; what is important is the fact that your thoughts turn from being self-conscious to being

God-conscious. A friend of mine says: "Every morning, as I awake, I lie there in my bed for a few moments and say to myself: 'When I open my eyes, the light comes in; when I open my mouth, the air comes in; when I open my heart, Christ comes in.'" Such thoughts help to prime the pump of the soul and cause the water of life to spring upwards into the day.

One of the things that deeply saddens me is the spirit of non-expectancy that seems to be so prevalent among so many Christians today. Many do not expect anything spiritually exciting in their day – they expect nothing more than just to muddle through. This is serious. You have only to look at certain countries in the Middle or Far East to see what the awful power of non-expectancy can do when it falls upon a civilisation. Whenever I visit these countries, I cannot help but notice how these otherwise lovely people respond so fatalistically to situations by turning over their hands in an attitude of helpless resignation.

The same danger lies at the door of the contemporary Christian Church. In some cases it has actually crossed the threshold and laid its paralysing hand upon the hearts of God's people, causing them to become resigned to spiritual defeat and failure. Dr Worcester, a medical practitioner who has worked in clinics among people who are troubled both in body and soul, says this astonishing thing: "Most Christians do not expect their religion to do them any great or immediate good. When one tells them that their condition need not last more than a single hour, they look at you as one who announces strange doctrine. They have become naturalised in defeat." How sad.

Spiritual expectancy

The first step to experiencing a spiritually profitable day is to expect a profitable day. Usually, those who expect nothing are not disappointed. They expect nothing spiritually exciting or profitable to happen to them, and that is mostly what they get. Such people think it utterly inconceivable that God should want to speak to them, guide them, or reveal Himself to them in some new and fresh way. They think of such experiences as being strange and abnormal. In fact, the Word of God makes it plain that God longs for this type of relationship with us. In John chapter 14: 23, Jesus says that if anyone loves Him, He and His Father "will come to him and make our home with him" (NIV).

John MacMurray, in his book *Reason and Emotion*, refers to the story of a little girl who was permanently lopsided and was brought to him for treatment. After working with her for some time, he managed to get her to stand quite straight. Then he asked her to walk across the room to her mother. She walked perfectly straight for the first time in her life and then, bursting into tears, threw herself into her mother's arms, crying, "Oh, Mummy, I'm walking all crooked!"

Christians who lack a spirit of expectancy are like that. They think of walking through the day with their heads held high and a song in their hearts as being something strange and unnatural. "Faith," said Dr Cynddylan Jones, a famous Welsh preacher, "is largely expectancy ... expectancy set on fire by the Holy Spirit." I promise you that if you begin your day by looking into your heavenly Father's face in a spirit of expectancy, you will not be disappointed. Learn to push expectantly on the gates of abundant living as you awake each morning, and as surely as day follows night, those gates will open wide.

Chapter 3

CULTIVATING CLOSENESS

"In the morning, O Lord, you hear my voice . . . I lay my requests before you and wait in expectation."
(Psalm 5:3, NIV)

I know of nothing that promotes the awareness of God's presence in a believer's life more powerfully and effectively than the regular practice of a morning Quiet Time.

Some have great difficulty with this, their lifestyle or circumstances prevent them from finding either the time or the place to be alone with God during the first part of the day. Don't feel condemned if your circumstances do not permit you to get alone with God until the day is well under way. He understands and will be there waiting for you whenever you can make it. The story is told of Susannah Wesley (the mother of John Wesley) that when, because of looking after her many children, she was deprived of privacy for her Quiet Time, she would lift her apron over her head, and for a few minutes commune in prayer with God. When the children saw her do this, they would whisper to each other, "Hush, mother is having her Quiet Time."

Try also to be alone when you have your Quiet Time. It is good for married couples to share together in prayer, but everyone needs to spend some time alone with God if they are to cultivate their individual relationship with Him. Every Christian must try to have some time alone with God at the beginning of the day, even if it is only a few quiet moments. Savour those moments, they will provide you with a fountain in your heart at which you can slake your thirst throughout the day.

Importance of regularity

In all the years I have been a Christian, I have never met anyone who told me that they enjoyed a deep and constant sense of God's presence who did not have fixed and regular times of prayer and contemplation.

I have met many who told me that after being baptised in the Holy Spirit, they felt such a keen sense of God's abiding presence in their lives that they no longer needed to spend fixed times with Him in prayer. One man put it like this: "Before I was filled with the Spirit, I used to have some pretty dull Quiet Times. Now I have a constant and continued 'Quiet Time' every moment I am awake. I no longer need to get alone with God in prayer or spend so much time in the Bible. I am more alive to God than I ever thought possible."

I warned him what would happen if he neglected fixed times with the Lord in prayer, and it was no surprise to hear a few months later that he had become spiritually cold and indifferent. Those who say that they can live in a state of strong spiritual awareness without definite times for prayer and contemplation will probably find themselves without both. It is about as senseless as saying that one can live in a state of physical nourishment without taking fixed times to eat. The times we set aside to cultivate an awareness of God result in a state of continual awareness of God. You can take it or leave it, but, believe me, life works best when you take it.

The New Testament tells us that Jesus felt the need of three simple habits: (1) He went into the synagogue to read "as his custom was"; (2) He went up a mountain to pray "as his custom was"; (3) He taught the people "as his custom was" (see Luke 4:16; Luke 22:39; Mark 10:1). These three simple habits of reading the Scriptures, spending time in prayer and sharing with others are as basic to the Christian life as "two and two make four" is to mathematics. If Jesus couldn't get along without definite times for prayer, then how can we hope to?

But how are we to make the best of our daily or regular times of prayer and contemplation? There can be no fixed rules, only suggestions. Experience has shown that the best way to begin a Quiet Time is by reading the Scriptures. This is why, now over twenty-five years ago, I began writing *Every Day with Jesus*. Prior to that, whenever I recommended people to begin their Quiet Time by reading the Word of God, they used to say: "But I don't know what to read." You cannot know the joy it gives me to know that thousands of people who hitherto had no daily Quiet Time now begin their day by reading the Word of God, followed by such booklets of devotional thoughts. My words, I know, help many, but they are not one-millionth as powerful and effective as the words of God. For through the Scriptures, Life speaks to life. God has gone into His Word and so, when we read it, God comes out of it.

Listening to God

After the reading of Scripture, one might sit quietly in the Lord's presence and say: "Father, have You anything to say to me?" Sometimes God may have something special and personal to say to you arising from your reading of His Word. Wait and see what He might have to say to you before moving on. A lady I know, who practises this approach, told me that when she says: "Father, have You anything to say to me?" the Lord sometimes responds: "No, nothing more than I have already said in my Word. But what have you to say to me?" God not only delights to talk to us, but He is delighted also when we talk to Him. This is what prayer is, a conversation with God. So talk to Him.

Tell Him the things that are on your mind, the joyful things as well as the difficult things.

If your mind wanders or gets distracted when you are praying, then pray about the thing to which your mind has wandered. Recently, while at prayer, I was distracted by an ambulance siren. I prayed, "Lord, whatever the problem is that sends this ambulance racing through the streets, be there to help and guide." The distraction became a direction. This is what is meant by bringing every thought into captivity to Christ (see 2 Corinthians 10:5).

One further suggestion, have a notebook and pen

near at hand when you begin your Quiet Time in case God says something to you. Had I not written down what came to me during my Quiet Times over the years, I would have been greatly deprived. A notebook can be a sign of faith. It says, "Speak, Lord, for your servant hears."

Chapter 4

COMPANIONSHIP

"'Remain in me, and I will remain in you.'"
(John 15:4, NIV)

Many years ago, an old Welsh miner told me that every day, following his Quiet Time, he would think of what he had to do that day and visualise the Lord as being involved in every moment of it. "I am in partnership with God," he said, "and I have learned to think of the responsibilities of the day not as 'mine', but as 'ours'." He ordered his day on the basis of a divine partnership.

He went on to tell me that as he thought ahead into the issues of the day, he would talk to God about them in the same way that a man would talk to a business partner: "What shall we do about this matter, Lord? There's another issue that will be coming up later in the day ... how shall we handle that? And then there is that other matter that just has to be completed today ... we need to be particularly careful about that, Father ... How shall we deal with it?" Jesus Himself said, "... live in me, and let me live in you ..." (John 15:4, TLB).

Divine – human partnership

The chief merit of this approach to practising the presence of God is that it highlights one of the greatest truths of Scripture, that of the divine-human partnership. Can you think of anything more wonderful in earth or heaven than the fact that the Almighty God, the Creator of the universe, takes an active interest in every single detail of our lives and is willing to team up with us? "Christianity," said a missionary to China, "is a secret companionship." Just think of it, you need not go into any day alone, but arm in arm with that Secret Companion. Some object to this idea on the basis that it makes us overdependent and prevents us from developing as persons. "God," they say, "has designed us to think for ourselves, and if we depend on the Almighty to do our thinking for us, we will not become free, self-determining, creative personalities."

There is some truth in this, of course, but as so often happens, if we take a part of a truth and do not consider the other parts, we will come out with wrong conclusions. Truth out of balance becomes error. Partnership with God does not mean that He dominates our personalities; His purpose is to guide, not override. The Almighty relates to us in a way that is helpful and supportive, yet, at the same time, taking care not to snuff out our initiative and creativity.

E. Stanley Jones describes the divine-human partnership in this way: "God comes close to His children in a way that leaves them free to think and act, yet in a way that awakens the personality to aliveness and alertness of mind and spirit. His guidance is always sufficiently obvious to be found, but not so obvious that it does away with the necessity of thought and discriminating insight." His secrets are always 'open secrets', open, yet sufficiently secret to make us think. This kind of partnership, to guide us without overriding us, is a task that only divine wisdom can accomplish. We would not expect anything less of the God who loves us, and anything else would be unworthy of Him.

Qualified role

If we are to go into every day on the basis of a divine-human partnership, then it might be helpful if we thought for a moment about God's qualifications for this important and significant role. We ask ourselves therefore: can the eternal God really understand the pressures and difficulties of living in the realm of time? Is He really able to enter into our human feelings?

The answer, of course, is 'yes'. In the person of His Son, God has worn our flesh, measured its frailty and knows exactly how we think and feel. A quaint old preacher was praying and thanking God for the Trinity, and when he came to Jesus, he said: "O God, even You couldn't do better than He did." There is no need to wonder what kind of partner God makes, for all you have to do is look at Jesus. He is, as someone put it, "God's highest character reference."

Let's look at some of the qualifications and characteristics of our divine Partner when He was here on earth, and see how eminently suitable He is for the role.

1. He was a person of immense courage: not the excited, desperate courage of the battlefield, but the quiet courage that went on in the face of growing opposition and certain crucifixion. Does the day ahead look as if it needs special courage and determination? Are you facing a situation that requires greater strength and confidence than you feel you are capable of? Then take heart, in Christ you have a Partner who knows precisely how you feel and will, if you ask Him, stamp His quiet courage and determination deep into your soul.

2. Can the great Creator of the universe really understand what goes on in the hearts and minds of finite human beings? The good news is that through the Incarnate Jesus, He does. However difficult our day might be, we have in Christ a Saviour and a Partner who knows and understands our deepest needs, and, what is more, He is able to provide the exact measure of strength and courage we require to meet what lies ahead.

3. He cares! When He was here on earth, He cared more about the needs of others than He did about His own needs. "'My food,' said Jesus, 'is to do the will of him who sent me and to finish his work'" (John 4:34, NIV). His care went beyond race, class or colour.

4. He gives! Whenever people consider entering into partnership with someone, they usually want to know how much their partner is willing to give. But the ultimate test of partnership is not just the giving of time, money, words, attendance at meetings, but the giving of oneself. Jesus Christ is that kind of partner; He gives more than words, He gives Himself. ". . . the Lord Jesus Christ . . . gave himself for our sins to rescue us from the present evil age, according to the will of our God and Father" (Galatians 1:3–4, NIV).

5. He empowers! The disciples, prior to Pentecost, were afraid that they might not be able to continue the work which Christ had committed to them but, after receiving the power of the Spirit, all that was changed. They were like men ablaze. Peter was clearly conscious that Christ had teamed up with them, for he said: ". . . what I do have I give you . . ." (Acts 3:6). You cannot give what you do not have. You have Christ and He has you. What better partner could you find in earth or in heaven?

Chapter 5

CHOOSING TO PRAISE

"But you are holy, who inhabit the praises
of Israel."
(Psalm 22:3, NKJ)

On reading the Bible, we are constantly reminded that God delights to dwell in the midst of His people's praise. On the basis of Psalm 22:3, I can promise you that the more you cultivate a praising heart, the more deeply you will feel the Lord's presence in your life.

Some might dislike my phrase "cultivating a praising heart" on the grounds that they believe praise must be spontaneous and not something that is called up from within the soul. It might be helpful if we were to begin by differentiating between two things, praise and thanksgiving. Although thanksgiving is a close relative of praise (they are often called 'the Siamese twins' of the Christian Church), they are quite distinct and separate in their meaning. We thank God for what He does but we praise Him for who He is. We might not always be able to find a reason to be thankful (though some would say we should), but we can always find a reason to praise. The Psalmist declared: "I will bless the Lord at all times; his praise shall continually be in my mouth" (Psalm 34:1, NKJ).

Continuous praise

Can we truly be expected to praise the Lord at all times? Surely it means "most times"? Or "almost all times"? The Psalmist is quite clear, "at all times". The prime purpose of praise is to honour and glorify God and because He never changes, then it follows that praise of Him is always appropriate. Some may feel they have little for which they can give thanks, but no one, no matter how poor, deprived or downcast, has any excuse not to praise.

Praise, unlike thanksgiving, begins not so much in the feelings as in the will. We can choose to praise the Almighty whether we feel like it or not. The Psalmist when he says, "O my God, my soul is cast down within me; therefore I will remember you . . ." (Psalm 42:6, NKJ), is obviously feeling downcast and disconsolate, and seems to find nothing in life for which he can be thankful. But look at how he deals with his doleful condition. Firstly, he admits to feeling downcast. He doesn't stay too long with his feelings, but he is careful not to deny them.

One of the greatest errors circulating in the Christian Church at the moment is the teaching that we must never admit to feeling down, for once we do we have given the devil the right to take over control in our lives. I have no hesitation in saying that this is sheer and utter nonsense, and has no support in Scripture.

After acknowledging his feelings, the Psalmist makes a choice: "I will remember you from the land of the Jordan, and from the heights of Hermon, from the hill Mizar" (Psalm 42:6, NKJ). He chooses to focus his thoughts, not on his downcast condition, but on the goodness of God in bringing His people into the Promised Land.

In the final verse of Psalm 42, he affirms a truth that every one of us would do well to focus on in times when we feel downcast, "Hope in God; for I shall yet praise him, the help of my countenance and my God" (NKJ). So whenever you feel sad or depressed, here's a secret that has taken me a lifetime to learn, acknowledge your feelings and then decide by an action of your will to focus your thought upon the goodness of God. Learn this now and, I promise you, it will save you from prolonged periods of gloom in the future.

Enabling health

A doctor once told me that the happiest and healthiest people are those who are quick to praise, not the flatterers or the insincere, but those who look for and quickly recognise the praiseworthy aspects of a situation. He was speaking of natural things but, as I listened to him, the thought came to me: if this is true in the natural realm, then how much more true will it be in the spiritual realm.

Dr Clyde Narramore defines praise as "inner health made audible". What does he mean? He means that there is a connection between a readiness to praise and the state of our physical health. If there really is this connection, then how can it be explained? I think one answer is that we are made in our innermost beings for praise. God designed us to be praising beings, and, when we praise, there is no surer way of completing and fulfilling ourselves. We are doing the very thing we were designed for.

I am sure you are familiar with this phrase from the Westminster Catechism: "Man's chief end is to glorify God and to enjoy Him for ever." If we decide not to make it our chief occupation to praise God (and remember once again, praise is a choice we can make), then inevitably we will suffer some spiritual and physical deprivation. A Christian physician says, "When I go through my day praising God, my blood flows better in my veins." Praise is good for you. It not only glorifies God but it makes you a better person. You will feel better, think better, work better, relate to others better and sleep better. Try it and see.

There are many reasons why we should praise God, not the least being the fact that when we do, we increase and sharpen the awareness of His presence in our lives. How is this so? Because the Lord inhabits the praises of His people. Praise is the ramp down which God comes running into our hearts. He delights so much in praise that when we reach out to Him in adoring worship, then, providing the praise and worship are genuine and not a covering up of some secret sin, He just cannot stay away.

Mechanical or medicinal

Can I ask you to determine right now that you will make it a daily habit to spend some time in praise of God? Once you make that commitment, then go further and decide how you will carry it out. Don't, whatever you do, leave it to the vagaries of feeling. A friend of mine has the kind of watch that can give out a bleep every hour, and he uses the time signal to prompt him to focus his thoughts on praising God. Another friend, who does quite a lot of driving, uses the moments when he is brought to a halt, in direct praise of God. A minister I know, whose telephone rings freqently, pauses for ten seconds before answering it, and uses those seconds in adoring praise. You might say that is mechanical. My friends tell me that it only sounds mechanical. They have found it to be medicinal. We pick up bad habits all too quickly. What is wrong with setting up a habit that enables us to turn our minds toward the Lord and give Him the praise which He so wondrously deserves?

Chapter 6

INNER
SEARCHING

*". . . clothe yourselves with the Lord Jesus Christ,
and do not think about how to gratify the desires
of the sinful nature."
(Romans 13:14, NIV)*

Nothing dulls or blunts the awareness of God's presence in our lives so much as continuing to think or act in ways of which God cannot approve. The harbouring of moral wrong makes God unreal.

Self analysis

In a church of which I once had the spiritual oversight, I knew a man who seemed to carry the sense of God's presence with him everywhere he went. People would often say that to spend a few minutes with him was a spiritual tonic. While visiting him in his home one day, I asked him to share with me the secret of his deep spirituality. At first, he was reluctant to discuss it, but after gentle probing, he told me that although he had a daily Quiet Time, early every Sunday morning he would get alone with God and examine his life in the light of five pointed questions:

(1) Have I been truthful and honest? (2) Have I been impure? (3) Have I allowed bitterness to take root in my heart? (4) Has love been my motive in everything? (5) Have I sought God's glory or my own glory?

It does no harm to consider these points ourselves:

1. Have I been truthful and honest?
"For we cannot do anything against the truth, but only for the truth" (2 Corinthians 13:8, NIV).

How do you and I stand in the light of that searching question today? You see, truth is inviolable. The early Christians, standing before tribunals, their lives in the balance, could have told a lie and their lives would have been saved. They refused, for they knew that truth was inviolable. They could die but they could not lie. Can you be depended on to tell the truth, no matter what the cost? Yes – or no? How easy it is to lie, even for a Christian; the willingness to twist a meaning to gain a point; to misquote if the misquotation serves an end; to exaggerate in order to impress. What is at the base of this looseness with the truth? It is often the fact that we believe a lie is justifiable. But it is not. We must remind ourselves once again that the truth is inviolable.

2. Have I been impure?
"You were bought at a price. Therefore honour God with your body" (1 Corinthians 6:20, NIV).

The question of purity is fundamental; if life sags at this point, it will probably sag all down the line. Have we victory or defeat at this point? I remember having to confront a church official on one occasion with some evidence of serious impurity, and, as he threw himself down into the chair in front of me, he said: "I may be guilty, but I am still a decent man. I am not a man of the gutter." Not of the gutter? Little did he realise it, but the gutter was in him! Those of us who have put ourselves under the authority of Christ must watch our tendency to excuse ourselves when caught up in some wrong. This might be a good moment to look into your heart and ask: am I a pure person? Do I allow my mind to dwell on things that blunt the awareness of Christ's presence in my life? If so, then surrender it now. Don't adopt the attitude of St Augustine, who once prayed: "Lord, make me pure, but not right now."

3. Have I allowed bitterness to take root in my heart? "See to it that no-one misses the grace of God and that no bitter root grows up ..." (Hebrews 12:15, NIV).

Of all the things that choke and poison spiritual growth, bitterness is probably the most devastatingly effective. Christ and bitterness are incompatible. If you hold on to bitterness, you have to let go of Christ, and if you hold on to Christ, you have to let go of bitterness. It is as simple as that. Each of us must ask ourselves at this very moment: am I a bitter person? Do I hold grudges? Do I find it hard to forgive? If so, then surrender it now into the hands of Christ. Give up your bitterness before it gets you down.

4. Has love been my motive in everything? "The love of Christ controls us ..." (2 Corinthians 5:14, RSV).

All the motives of life, if they are to be sound, are reduced to one, love. And this love is not a general love, but a specific one, the love of Christ. This cuts deep. It is possible to be controlled by the love of achievement, of success, of a cause, of one's fight. To be controlled by the love of Christ is different, not only in degree, but in kind and quality. When we do everything for the love of Christ, it transforms the menial into the meaningful, the sordid into the sacred. Perhaps this, more than any other thing, makes the presence of God alive in our hearts. Listen to what the apostle John says about that: "Now he who keeps his commandments abides in him, and he in him" (1 John 3:24, NKJ).

5. Have I sought God's glory, or my own glory?
"... whatever you do, do it all for the glory of God" (1 Corinthians 10:31, NIV).

This, too, cuts deep. In the last analysis, what prompts your actions, self-interest or Christ-interest? In the deepest citadel of your spirit, who has the final word, you or Christ? For you see, the issue is this: if you dominate your life, then Christ cannot dominate it. You will not feel His presence as strongly in your heart. You will be more self-conscious than Christ-conscious.

I am not suggesting that the five questions my friend asked himself should be used continually by everyone. That is something that he found helpful but the Lord may lead you in another direction. What is important, however, is that we are willing occasionally to expose ourselves to some form of self-examination or spiritual check-up. And not just examine ourselves, but decide to do something about the things we discover which are blunting the edge of our spiritual awareness.

Letting go

A minister's little daughter went into a guest's room and stole some sweets. When challenged by her mother as to where she got them, she told her first lie. The broken-hearted mother put her on her lap and told her what it all meant. The little girl wept bitterly and the mother said: "I'm glad to see you are sorry, now take the sweet out of your mouth and throw it away." The little girl looked at her mother through her tears, clamped her mouth shut and said, "No, I am enjoying it too much." She didn't like to be guilty of wrongdoing, and even wept over it; she did everything except the one thing that was necessary, give it up.

Chapter 7

PRAYING THE AFFIRMATIVE WAY

"The Lord is with me; he is my helper."
(Psalm 118:7, NIV)

Praying the affirmative way is not a phrase that appears very often in modern-day devotional literature, but the concept underlying it is a Biblical one nevertheless. Praying the affirmative way is not asking for something to be so, but affirming it to be so; it is proclaiming to oneself that a matter or an issue is exactly the way God has decreed it.

You see, there are some things in the Christian life that we do not need to ask for at all, they are part and parcel of our Christian commitment. And the promise of God's continued presence is one of them. Listen to what the Almighty says concerning this tremendous fact. "I will never leave you nor forsake you" (Hebrews 13:5, NKJ). And again: "When my father and my mother forsake me, then the Lord will take care of me" (Psalm 27:10, NKJ).

On the basis of these verses, and there are many more, once we surrender our lives to God and are His committed sons and daughters, then we have the guarantee that His presence will be in and around us every moment of the day. So do not ask for it, affirm it. Instead of praying: "O God, be with me through every moment of this day," say: "Thank You, Father, that You are with me right now." You may withdraw from Him, but He will never withdraw from you.

There are some things in life, concerning which we would have to say in all honesty, that we are not sure whether we know the mind of God about them. Thus we pray and petition God for light and illumination before we can proceed. But no Christian need be unsure of God's promise to dwell in the hearts of those who are His children. He has put the issue beyond all possible doubt by assuring us, as Psalm 91:1 assures us, "We live within the shadow of the Almighty . . ." (TLB), that He is ever with us.

Abusing God's blessing

Why, then, do we find ourselves so often praying for God to be with us, instead of simply affirming it? One reason could be that we have a concern not to take the blessings and favours of God for granted. I suppose most of us, to varying degrees, are aware that we tend to take the blessings of God more for granted than with gratitude; so, to avoid doing this, we lean the other way and concentrate on asking God to give us something which He has already vouchsafed, namely His continued presence. This is a kind of compensation in which we go to one extreme in order to avoid another. Someone has described it as "leaning backward to avoid tipping forward". Can you see what I mean? It may sound very "spiritual" to ask God to surround us with His presence, but when we look more deeply into our motives, we may find that the real reason why we do it is because we do not really believe His word of promise in the first place. Is this too hard and judgmental? I think not. We must be careful not to rationalise spiritual issues; it is far better to acknowledge that this may be a possibility, and consider it, rather than dismiss it out of hand. So ask yourself now: do I believe that Christ's presence is with me every moment of the day? If your answer is "Yes", then ask yourself this further question: then why do I not more frequently affirm it?

Let's consider a second reason why we do not pray the affirmative way: because we do not clearly understand the difference between petition and affirmation. The difference, quite simply, is this: petition is asking God for something, affirmation is acknowledging that we have it. There are times when it is right to petition God, and there are times when it is wrong. Where is the dividing line? I suggest it centres on two things: (1) that God wants to give us what we ask for, and (2) that it is His perfect time. When both of these are in agreement, we need no longer ask, we simply believe it.

Now apply these suggestions to the question of God's presence. Do we know He wants to give it to us? The answer is "Yes". Is it dependent on a certain time? No, He has pledged never to leave us. Why ask for something that we know God wants to give us and never takes away? So, as far as the matter of God's presence is concerned, do not ask for it, affirm it.

45

Exercising faith

We must spend a little more time discussing the difference between the prayer of petition and the prayer of affirmation. The truth is, in relation to this matter of the presence of God, we need not petition Him at all. This may seem, as we said, that we are taking His presence for granted, but really it isn't. We are simply taking God at His word. Some might think all this is a quibble about words, and will say, "What does it matter how we frame our prayers? God knows what we mean. After all, a loving, earthly father would not get upset with a child who phrases his statements incorrectly. A father's love overlooks all that." That is quite true, but the issue needs to be looked at, not so much from God's side, but from ours. You see, the statements of Scripture that show God's presence is always with us demand of us a degree of faith, and faith, generally speaking, is not something we are very good at displaying. We would much prefer not to have to exercise faith and believe that God means what He says by praying in such words as these: "Lord, help me to believe that Your presence is with me everywhere I go."

I know full well that there are times when we have to pray like that, when our faith is weak and we are going through a hard and difficult time. But what I am advocating is exercising our faith so that, more and more, we begin to take God at His word. If we can't affirm the thing which the Lord has made crystal clear in the Bible, such as His constant and continued presence, then how are we going to grow in faith so that we can affirm those things which are not so clear?

Chapter 8

A CONSTANT CLOSENESS

*"'And surely I am with you always, to the very
end of the age.'"
(Matthew 28:20, NIV)*

In a previous chapter, I referred to the idea of setting
up habits that remind us of the need to praise, but
now I want to talk about establishing some habits that
will help remind us of the nearness of our Master's
presence. These practices might not appeal to everyone, but those who follow them say they have greatly
helped in bringing about a sharper awareness of
God's presence in their lives.

Increasing awareness

Dr Frank Laubach, a medical practitioner who has
made a lifelong study of the methods which Christians
follow to increase their awareness of God's presence,
says that some of the most popular ones are these:
walking on the inside of the pavement and visualis-
ing the Lord walking on the kerb side; playing the
game of "Minutes", in which you see how many

times during an hour you think of God, then counting the number of minutes that you thought about Him; taking a breath and saying: "As this physical breath I am taking is filling my whole body with life-giving oxygen, so the breath of God, when I take it in, strengthens and sustains my inner life."

Paul Bexon, one of the managers at CWR, says that this last suggestion is one that he sometimes follows – taking slow, steady breaths while sitting quietly in God's presence, and using that as a physical focus to remind us that the Almighty is closer than the very air we breathe. Can I suggest that you pause for a moment of quietness right now, take a few deep breaths and say the following prayer:

My Father and my God, as this physical breath I am taking is cleansing the blood in my lungs from all impurities, so Your breath, as I take it within my being, purifies my inner life. I am so very, very grateful. Amen.

Another daily practice or habit which some people establish as a reminder that God's presence is always with them (especially those who live alone) is to leave a vacant chair at a table or at the bedside and imagine Christ sitting there. A minister, when visiting a Christian woman who had previously complained to him that she was lonely, gave her this suggestion: "Every morning, when you have your coffee, pull up a chair and imagine that the Lord is sitting there with you. Talk to Him. Tell Him everything – your joys, your sorrows, your views on life and so on." At first, she reacted strongly against his advice, classifying it as "unhelpful and unspiritual", but later she did as he suggested. When the minister visited her some weeks later, he found a transformed woman. She said, "That advice has helped me more than you will ever know. I have my Quiet Time early in the morning, when I read God's Word and pray, nothing can eclipse that, but I enjoy so much those moments when the Lord and I have our "elevenses" together. Precisely at 11 a.m., I pull up two chairs at my kitchen table, pour out two cups of coffee, one for me and one for the Lord, and then we enjoy a lovely chat together. And sometimes we get so carried away that we even forget to drink our coffee!"

A missionary who lived alone and had a strong tendency to worry used to pull up a chair alongside his bed at night and imagine Christ sitting there. Someone who knew of this habit once asked him: "John, what does the Lord say to you in those closing moments before you fall asleep?" He replied: "He says, 'You go to sleep now, John, and I'll stay up.'"

Spiritual crutches

I confess that, for many years, I viewed some of the habits and practices we have been discussing as nothing more than "crutches" for those who would not give priority to daily Bible reading and prayer. As I have talked with devout Christians about their spiritual lives, however, I have had to change my mind about this, for I have seen how, in addition to regular Bible reading and prayer, the establishing of a simple, daily habit has made their relationship with God even more meaningful.

49

We look now at another habit which some people practise in order to remind themselves of God's continuing presence in their lives, being alert and watching for anything interesting or unusual that happens during the day, and immediately bringing God into it. One woman I know, who practises this, says: "Whenever something unusual or unexpected happens in my day, such as bumping into an old friend I haven't seen for years, receiving an unexpected 'phone call or a surprise gift, I immediately relate all such happenings to God, and say: 'Lord, how lovely of You to arrange my day in this way.' I have done this so often that now it has become a fixed habit, one that immediately focuses my mind on His all-pervading presence." Stay alert and watch out for the unusual and the unexpected, and let it trigger off in you an appreciation and an awareness of your Lord's constant presence in your life.

Thanksgiving

We look at one last daily practice or habit which can be used as a reminder of the constancy of our Lord's presence in our lives. It is the practice of letting every completed task become a trigger for approaching God and thanking Him for the gift of His presence.

Some years ago, a woman who was seriously depressed came to me for counselling, and told me that the cause of her depression was her husband's lack of interest in their home and in her personally. "I can clean the house from top to bottom," she said, "and my husband will not notice a thing. This makes me so angry, but nothing seems to change him, not even when I get depressed." After working with her for a few weeks, I suggested to her that the next time she cleaned the house, she should get down on her knees and say: "Lord, thank You for this home You have given me. I have cleaned it from top to bottom for You. Though my husband may not appreciate it, I know You do. You are with me in everything I do." When she cleaned her house a few days later, she did what I suggested and was amazed to hear the Lord say to her: "Well done." Those two words wiped out her depression, for it had developed largely from her perception that no one was interested in her. Now I cannot promise, whenever you finish a task and turn to God in prayer, that you will hear His voice so clearly, but I can promise that He will find some secret stair into your soul. God delights in our response to Him and, believe me, His eye is quick to detect an appreciation for His presence.

Chapter 9

BIBLICAL MEDITATION

"Be still, and know that I am God . . ."
(Psalm 46:10, NIV)

We pause at the beginning of this chapter to remind ourselves of what we understand and mean when we talk about practising the presence of God. It is the fixing of the soul's gaze upon God, the savouring of Him, the remembering of His unimpeachable promise that "I will never leave you nor forsake you". Brother Lawrence defined it in this way, "The unbroken attitude of mind which envisages God within, the hearer of all speech, the monitor of all thoughts, the judge of all actions."

Since we can easily lose sight of the fact that God is with us in everything we do, we need to pause from time to time and direct our thoughts and our gaze toward Him. And the more often we can do this, the more deeply aware of Him we will become. So we ask ourselves once more: what else can we do to deepen and enhance our awareness of our Lord's promised presence in our lives?

A lost art

Another way of practising His presence is through *Biblical meditation*. This is, without doubt, one of the greatest ways we can ever discover of realising God's presence in our lives, but, regrettably, it is one that is little understood and little used. David Ray, an American minister and author, says: "I used to look with suspicion on people who talked about Bible meditation as being out of touch with reality. Then someone showed me how to take a verse such as Psalm 46:10, 'Be still, and know that I am God' (NIV), and allow it to soak into my thoughts. Within days, I became more aware of God's presence in my life than ever before."

May I suggest that you begin right now to practise the art of Bible meditation by letting this same verse lie on your mind throughout the day. If necessary, put down this book, think about the verse, probe it, contemplate it, and draw from it all that God has put into it, view it from every angle, ponder on it, letting it affect the deepest parts of your being.

Bible meditation must not be confused with other types of meditation, particularly those that come out of the East. Other forms of meditation focus on emptying the mind; Bible meditation focuses on filling it – filling it with the truths and insights of Scripture. If there is one thing that continues to surprise and astonish me, it is the fact that although the Bible has so much to say about meditation, only a minority understand and practise it. A research conducted among Christians in the United States of America showed that comparatively few knew how to meditate. What percentage do you think it was? One in ten? No. One in a hundred? No. One in a thousand? No. Only one in ten-thousand knew how to meditate.

Now get this, for it could be a watershed in your Christian experience. You can read the Bible, memorise the Bible, study the Bible, but unless you know how to meditate on it, you will not get the best out of it. Reading, memorising and studying the Bible are excellent disciplines. They are to be encouraged and applauded. But the Christian who does no more than read it, memorise it and study it is like a person who chews his food but doesn't swallow it. Proverbs 12:27, "The lazy man does not roast his game ..." (NIV), shows just what we are like when we fail to meditate.

Rumination

One of the synonyms for the word "meditate" is "ruminate". Many animals, such as sheep, goats, antelope, camels, cows and giraffe are called ruminant animals. This is because they have stomachs with several compartments, the first of which is called the *rumen*. The way a ruminant animal digests its food is fascinating. First it literally bolts it down and then later regurgitates it from the rumen back into its mouth, where it is chewed again to extract further nourishment from the food. This process of rumination, or chewing the cud, enables the food to be thoroughly digested, whereupon it is absorbed into the animal's bloodstream, so becoming part of its life.

Rumination and meditation are parallel words.

Now follow me carefully here: when a Christian takes a text or phrase of the Bible and quietly and continuously contemplates it, the power and energy that is contained in the Word of God is absorbed into the spirit, the motivating centre of the personality. You see, the mind is not the most important part of us; the spirit is the most important part. Truth held in the mind must become assimilated by the spirit if it is to have its greatest influence and effect. Some truth reaches the spirit from that which is held in the mind, but the more we contemplate and meditate on Scripture, the more speedily, the more effectively and the more powerfully is truth impressed into our spirit. Just as a ruminant animal gets its nourishment and energy from the grass through the process of rumination, so, through meditation, a Christian extracts from Scripture the life and energy that God has put into it.

How to begin

I want you to take a text and begin to practise the art of meditation. Jesus said, "If you live your life in me, and my words live in your hearts, you can ask for whatever you like and it will come true for you" (John 15:7, J.B. Phillips). The first thing you must do, of course, is to memorise it. This should not take you long, but if you have any difficulty in remembering a verse of Scripture, write it on a card which you keep in your pocket, and refer to it as often as you can throughout the day.

Now begin meditating on it. This means bringing it into the central focus of your mind at different times throughout the day. Think about what it is saying. Ponder it, probe it with questions such as these: "If you live your life in me" – I wonder what that means? What does it mean to live in Christ? What life is the Lord talking about here, natural life or spiritual life? What more ought I to be doing to "live" in Him? Then go on to the next phrase: "And my words live in your hearts." What does that mean? What words is Christ talking about here? How many "words" of Christ do I know? How many have I memorised?

Got the idea? Now go on and contemplate the next phrase: "You can ask for whatever you like and it will come true for you." "Whatever you like" – does that mean I can get anything I want out of God? No, for if His word is living in my heart then I will only ask for those things that are in accordance with His will; my spirit will be so in tune with Him that I will only want what He wants. I rarely make promises or give guarantees, but I can guarantee this: if you take a verse of Scripture like this each day of your life and meditate on it, then, other things being equal, you will never have to wonder why you can't feel God's presence in your heart and life.

Chapter 10

MEETING WITH GOD

*"For where two or three come together in my
name, there am I . . ."*
(Matthew 18:20, NIV)

His presence in fellowship

We turn now to consider a way of practising the
presence of God that all believers follow except, of
course, those who are housebound by reason of
sickness or infirmity. I refer to the matter of *meeting
together in fellowship with other Christians*. All of us do
this, but not all of us understand the power and
significance of what happens when we meet together
in our Lord's Name. Although the presence of Christ
is with every Christian individually, whenever we
meet together corporately for prayer and worship,
the presence of the Lord seems to be more intensely
felt within ourselves individually. Why should this
be? One reason is, I think, that in the process of
opening up our spirits to one another, we automatically
open up more of our spirit to God. This has been
something that has intrigued me for many years, for I

have discovered that the more effort I have made to relate to my brothers and sisters in Christ, the closer I seem to get to God. It is as if, in the physical presence of other Christians, praying together, singing together, sharing together, something is triggered that opens one's spirit more to God.

C.S. Lewis once expressed a similar thought: "God can only show Himself as He really is . . . to men (and women) who are united together in a body, loving one another, helping one another, showing Him to one another . . . consequently the only really adequate instrument for learning about God is the whole Christian community, waiting for Him together." The closer we get to each other, the closer we will get to God, and the closer we get to God, the closer we will want to get to each other. This concept is something that we ought to be more aware of and pay more attention to in the contemporary Christian Church.

You see, if we do not take the necessary steps to experience true Christian fellowship, then we inevitably deprive ourselves of the joy of His corporate presence. God can only mediate His presence in and through a community of His people to the extent that they are open to Him and to one another. I know a number of churches where the people belong to a common tradition, subscribe to a common creed, share a common form of doctrine, but do not belong to each other. They think that sharing common beliefs makes them a living fellowship, but it doesn't.

A sharing fellowship

What makes a group of Christians a living fellowship is their desire and willingness to open up to one another and to share on the deepest levels of their personalities. Children who do not feel they "belong" in a family are usually troubled children. What is it like in your church? Is it a place where you feel you really "belong", belong not just to Christ but to one another? If so, then rejoice in it. If not, then begin to share yourself with your brothers and sisters as deeply as you are able. A church where people have no true relationship with each other blocks the way for the mediation of God's corporate presence. God can only mediate His presence to the degree that His people are willing to open themselves up to Him and to one another. The only exception I know to this is during times of revival, when God flows into a group of people in such terrible and awesome power that He sweeps aside all obstacles and hindrances.

I heard just recently of a church where the leaders and the congregation, recognising that they were not experiencing the degree of Christ's presence in their meetings that they should, got together one Saturday for a time of self-examination. As they shared openly with one another, it was obvious that there were many barriers between them. They were courageous enough to identify them and make a list of them: fears, suspicions, jealousies, resentments, guilts, self-preoccupations, a desire to have one's own way, resistance to God-given authority and so on.

The list was put up on an overhead projector and they said: "These are the things that keep us from one another." Someone then asked: "What shall we do?" A decision was made to break down into small groups and give several hours a week to the task of building better relationships with each other. It was a very cleansing process, a catharsis. Then what happened? I am sure you will have guessed – God made His presence felt so powerfully in their midst that it moved them into a new dimension of spiritual authority and power. We must not get the impression, however, from what we have been saying that all we need to do to realise Christ's presence in a corporate way is to relate only with each other. This would put the focus on us, and not on Him.

Christ-centred fellowship

One of the problems that can arise in churches where there is a strong relational focus is that of concentrating more on the horizontal relationship than on the vertical relationship. We must never forget that it is in Christ's Name that we meet, not in our own name. No matter how good our horizontal relationships, if we lose sight of the fact that we are to focus more on Christ than ourselves, we will never experience the presence of Christ in the way we should. After all, what gives a Christian congregation cohesion? What holds it together? It is not just the presence of Christ, but the Person behind the presence, Christ Himself.

In the days when I was a pastor in Yorkshire and used to visit my flock, an old lady would always remark as I bade her farewell by her garden gate: "I will see you at the next meeting, for I don't want to miss meeting Him." Most people would have said: "I will see you at the next meeting." But her focus was not just on meeting with her fellow Christians – "them"; it was meeting with her Lord – "Him". She loved "them", but she loved "Him" even more. Our priorities in our times of Christian fellowship together must be in that order, first "Him" and then "them". Whenever we link ourselves with "Him", we have one of the greatest means of practising the presence of God that we can ever know.

What other options are there open to us for increasing our awareness of the presence of God in our lives? I use the word "options" because we can take them or leave them; God will not force them upon us. He makes Himself available to us, and when we make ourselves available to Him, the result will be a deep and continuous sense of His presence in our hearts.

Spirit filled fellowship

Another way, then, in which we can heighten the awareness of God's presence in our beings is found in Ephesians 5:18, ". . . be filled with the Spirit" (NIV). One of the ministries of the Holy Spirit is to make God and His Son, Jesus Christ, real to us: "He (the Holy Spirit) will glorify me, for he will take of what is mine and declare it to you" (John 16:14, NKJ). It follows, therefore, that the more we allow the Holy Spirit to have sway in our lives, the more aware we will be of the divine presence.

Now the question will be asked: what does it mean to be filled with the Spirit? Does not every Christian possess the Holy Spirit? The answer is "Yes", for

Scripture teaches that every Christian has the Holy Spirit from the moment of their conversion. Take this text, for example: "Unless one is born of water and the Spirit, he cannot enter the kingdom of God" (John 3:5, NKJ). However, although all Christians have the Holy Spirit, the Holy Spirit doesn't have all Christians. They may have Him, but He doesn't have them. In the light of this, can I ask you to face this question with me before going any further: I have the Holy Spirit, but does He really have me?

Chapter 11

TRANSFORMED
BY GOD

*". . . But you know him, for he lives with you and
will be in you."
(John 14:17, NIV)*

If every Christian has the Holy Spirit, then why do
we have this continuous debate among ourselves
about such phrases as "the baptism of the Spirit",
"being filled with the Spirit", "walking in the Spirit",
and so on?

I thought long and hard about this in the early days
of my Christian experience, but it was not until I was
shown the three different prepositions which Jesus
used in relation to the Holy Spirit that the matter
became clear to me. Someone has said: "A preposition can alter a proposition," and nowhere is that
more true than in relation to the teaching on the Holy
Spirit. Get your prepositions right and you will have
no difficulty with the propositions.

The three prepositions

When Jesus talked about the Holy Spirit, He used
these three prepositions – **with, in** and **upon**. Let's

look at each of these in turn. What did Jesus mean when He said the Holy Spirit was **with** the disciples? He meant, so I believe, that the Spirit was accompanying them, was working with them on the outside. He most certainly was not in them, for Christ clearly indicated that that phase of the Spirit would be at some point in the future: "He will be in you."

This is how the Spirit worked in our lives, prior to our conversion. He was with us in order to convict us of sin and to persuade us of the fact that without Christ, our eternal future was one of gloom and despair. Wonderful and awesome though it may be to have the Spirit with us, there can be no real or radical change in our lives until the Holy Spirit moves within us. This brings us to the question: when did the Holy Spirit enter into the disciples in order to regenerate them and bring them into the experience of the new birth? Many people will say that it took place at Pentecost. I do not think so myself, and let me tell you why.

John chapter 20:19–31 depicts that glorious post-resurrection meeting of Christ with His disciples in which, after commissioning them, He proceeded to breathe on them, saying: "Receive the Holy Spirit" (verse 22, NIV). What did the disciples receive at that moment? Obviously the Holy Spirit. But if that is so, then what happened on the Day of Pentecost? Was that a double portion of the Spirit? This is where our prepositions help. Here in the locked room where Jesus appeared, I believe the disciples' hearts were regenerated by the power of the Holy Spirit. He who had been **with** them to accompany them, now came **in** them to convert them.

Although the disciples belonged to Christ prior to the Cross and resurrection, they could not have actually experienced the regenerative power of the Spirit, for that could only have been conveyed to them following Christ's conquest of Satan on the Cross and His victory over the grave. It is interesting that the first thing Jesus does when meeting His disciples, after coming back from the dead, is to impart to them the Holy Spirit. Now, because of the Cross and resurrection, He who had been with them was able to come into them.

We look now at the third preposition which Jesus used in relation to the Holy Spirit: "You shall receive power when the Holy Spirit has come upon you" (Acts 1:8, NKJ). This was a prophetic reference to a day not far distant, the Day of Pentecost, when the Spirit would once again have a part to play in their lives.

So now we must ask ourselves: what happened at Pentecost? The Holy Spirit, who had been **with** the disciples prior to the Cross and resurrection, and who came **in** them in the Upper Room, would now come **upon** them in all His fullness to saturate them with divine power and turn them from timid, vacillating disciples into men and women who were ablaze and invincible. And did that happen? Let the facts speak for themselves. When the Spirit came in fullness at Pentecost, the disciples, who hitherto, though converted and committed to Christ, were somewhat frightened and dispirited, began to feel His personal presence in a way that transformed them within. Now they had no doubt that Christ was actually living in their lives and, feeling His personal presence with them, they went out and began to turn the world upside down.

What has all this to do with what we are saying? This – though the Spirit has been **with** you in order to bring you to Christ, and is now **in** you through the work of regeneration, the question remains: have I experienced my own personal Pentecost and know the Spirit clothing me, enduing me with divine energy and power? Whatever your view or interpretation of the Holy Spirit, the bottom line is this – is He a dynamic or merely a doctrine?

Chapter 12

LIVING FOR GOD

*". . . I urge you . . . to offer your bodies as living
sacrifices, holy and pleasing to God . . ."*
(Romans 12:1, NIV)

We turn to consider an aspect of practising the
presence of God that to some may seem incongruous,
but, I believe, it is an issue which, if kept in its proper
perspective, plays a vital part in maintaining a heightened awareness of God's presence in our lives. I
refer to the matter of *keeping the physical body, as far as
possible, in good health and order.* I say "as far as
possible" because some are handicapped with a poor
physical frame. Even so, perhaps it can be made
better, even well.

Temple of the Holy Spirit

Our physical body is the house in which the soul
lives, and if, through neglect or abuse, we allow that
house to fall into disrepair, it might well have an
adverse affect upon the soul. Just as what goes on in
the soul can influence and affect what goes on in the

body, so what goes on in the body can influence and affect what goes on in the soul.

Down the centuries, there have always been those who have looked on the body as the enemy of the soul. They see it as something that has to be continually suppressed, sometimes mutilated, and they go through life lamenting the fact that their soul is imprisoned in a body. I heard one Christian say about another: "He seems to be ashamed that he inhabits his body."

There is not one word of Scripture that leads us to have a morbid view of our bodies. On the contrary, the passage at the head of this chapter exhorts us to present our *bodies* as a living sacrifice. Note the word "living". While we are here on earth, we live in a body, whether we like it or not. Better not to deny the fact, and work to ensure that, as far as we are able, our bodies become a well-kept temple in which the presence of God can effectively dwell (see 1 Corinthians 6:19–20). The Bible teaches, of course, that the body has been affected by the Fall and that the curse, which fell on the earth, has greatly affected our physical functioning, but it encourages us, nevertheless, to respect our bodies and view them as a temple in which the presence of God dwells.

Jesus accepted His body as a gift from God: "A body You have prepared for me" (Hebrews 10:5, NKJ). His body and soul were attuned. He neither neglected His body nor pampered it, He offered it as the vehicle of God's will and purpose. It is Jesus Christ, and not sick or infirm saints (no disrespect intended), who must be the pattern of how we are to act toward our bodies. Just enough sleep to make us fresh, and a little less than that which would make us lazy. Just enough food to keep us fit and not make us fat. Just enough physical exercise for fitness and not so much that we become so preoccupied with it that it drains higher interests.

If we keep our bodies fit like a well-tuned violin, then the music of God will be able to come forth from every fibre of our being. So when tempted to ignore the needs of our body, say to yourself: "No, this cannot be; my body is a temple of the Holy Spirit and deserves my highest concentration and interest." Not long ago, I stood outside a cathedral which had a large notice board displaying the words: "Divine service is held here for one hour every day." I said to a friend who was with me: "There ought to be a sign on every Christian's body that says, 'Divine service is held here 24 hours a day!'"

Fit for the Almighty

If the body is the temple in which God dwells, then what can we do to make it a fit habitation for the Almighty? You will need to keep in mind that I am not going to refer here to emotional things, but to things that are purely physical. It is true that our emotions and attitudes greatly affect our physical functioning but, as I am going to deal with these issues a little later on, my concern now is to focus purely and simply on the matter of physical care.

First, if you have not done so for a long time, have a physical check-up to see if there are any structural problems in your body. If there aren't, then you know that you can give yourself in a disciplined way

71

to some of the other things I am going to mention. Second, make sure you have plenty of physical exercise. I have said this to thousands of people in seminars and in my writings, that when I maintain a regular programme of physical exercise, I find I can write better, think better and concentrate better. When I let up on my exercise programme, I find that it takes a few extra hours a day to complete my tasks.

Third, control your appetite. A traveller tells of how he watched a man on board ship, pacing up and down like a caged tiger, irritable and out of sorts because his breakfast had not come on time. He didn't just have an appetite; the appetite had him. In addition to that, says the traveller, the man was fifty pounds overweight. If you are overweight, then try this as an exercise: put your hands on the table when you are halfway through a meal, and push so hard that your chair moves away from the table. It is one of the best weight-reducing techniques I know.

Fourth, learn to relax. I once attended a seminar on the subject of relaxation. It was one of the most profitable things I have ever done. This is what I do whenever I feel tense and under stress. I lie down on a bed, close my eyes and say to all the organs of my body in succession: "Brain, you are now in the presence of God. Let go and listen. He wants to touch you. Receive His peace. Eyes, you are weary through looking at many distracting things. You are now in the presence of the One who made you. Receive His peace. Nerves, you who are the intelligence department of my being, strained and torn by living in a world of chaos, you are now to report better news. God is coming to you with the news of calmness and tranquillity. Receive His peace." I go over my whole body like this, which takes about ten or fifteen minutes. Often I rise as if made anew.

Fifth, build into your life periods of recreation. By this I mean activities that leave you physically rejuvenated and toned up. Life must have periods of creation and recreation. All creation and no recreation makes "Jack", and everyone else, a dull boy. Life is made for work and play. Recreation, whether it is a physical game or a mental game, must leave you with a sense of heightened vitality in the total being. And remember, any recreation into which Christ cannot be taken is not for a Christian. Follow these guidelines, and they will help prevent your body from dampening the delights of the presence of God in your soul.

Chapter 13

A MIND FOR GOD

*"He restores my soul; he leads me in the paths of
righteousness for his name's sake."
(Psalm 23:3, NKJ)*

Having looked at the need to keep our physical body
in as good order as possible, so that it does not
adversely affect our spiritual sensitivity, we turn our
attention now to *the realm of the mental and emotional.*
Did you know that wrong mental attitudes and
unhealed hurts can reverberate inside you to such a
degree that they can sometimes effectively suppress
the sense of God's presence within your soul?

Inner wounds

When I came into the Christian ministry, in the early
1950s, I found that, despite my theological training,
there were some people whom I could not help. They
were the ones who came to me and said something
like this: "I know I am a Christian, but there are times
when God's presence seems to leave me, and I am
overcome by feelings of deep loneliness and sadness.

I have not committed sin, and I know of nothing in my life that is dishonouring to God. These feelings seem to come out of nowhere and without any apparent reason. I do not know what to do about them. Can you help me?"

I don't mind telling you that, when faced with a question like that, I was completely and hopelessly lost. Then I stumbled upon the answer. Many of these people were feeling this way because of some unhealed hurt of the past, some disturbing memory that had been repressed, or some wrong attitude that had never been corrected. These things rose up from time to time within the soul and blunted their spiritual sharpness and sensitivity. If you have ever experienced what I am talking about, then I hope that what I am going to say over the next few pages may help you to control this problem whenever it occurs again.

You can be walking along the street with a deep awareness of Christ's presence in your life when, without warning and for no apparent reason, a dark cloud descends upon the soul and dampens your spiritual delight. One of the major causes of this is that something out of your past, a repressed fear, an unhealed hurt, a deep rejection has intruded into the present, taking its toll on the personality.

A few years ago, someone said to me: "There are times when I feel God's presence surrounding me so closely that I feel like dancing with joy, and then suddenly, for some reason, I feel incredibly lonely. Why is this?" I was not able to spend much time with this person, but a few pointed questions brought us both to see that in that person's spirit was a wound that had never been healed.

But what is a wounded spirit? We usually think of wounds occurring in battles or during a fight, but the spirit can equally be wounded, and these wounds are sometimes deeper and more painful than a physical wound. The wounds I am talking about here usually arise from two things, deep hurts and deep horrors. The hurts come from rejection or deprivation of love. The horrors come from having experienced deep trauma, brutality, violence and physical abuse. Can Christ really sympathise and help us with our deep inner wounds? He can!

Dealing with the past

In some Christian circles, thankfully not all, whenever the subject of past problems intruding into the present is mentioned, the objection is raised: "What are you doing? Are you denying the power and reality of conversion? All those things are dealt with at the moment a person is converted, so why harp back to the past?"

If there is one thing that has caused great difficulty in the Christian Church, it is the teaching that conversion instantly resolves all our emotional problems. It simply is not true. It is true that, at conversion, we have the potential for dealing with all our emotional problems; and it is also true that, at conversion, some people have been healed of all their emotional problems; but it is definitely not true that it happens automatically. We cannot begin to help each other until we are willing to face reality and deal with issues, not as we would like them to be, but as they are. But how is a wounded spirit healed? What must we do to overcome these problems of the past that sometimes intrude into the present and blunt the edge of our spiritual awareness?

First, we have to face the fact that these things are going on within us. Don't hide from it and say, "All this was dealt with at my conversion and I am just deceiving myself that I have a problem." This kind of difficulty cannot be dealt with by wishful thinking. So acknowledge it to yourself, and, if you can, share it with another Christian, preferably a counsellor. I would not have said this many years ago, but experience has shown me that many Christians miss out on healing because they are unwilling to share something with another person.

The second thing we ought to do is to accept some responsibility for the way we are. But you say: "I was the one who was rejected, deprived and subjected to the most terrifying trauma. You just don't know what happened to me." That may be true, but, in every situation we face in life, we have the choice to respond either in a forgiving way or a resentful way. What I am saying now might sound hard and insensitive, but, believe me, no one can be freed of these things from the past until they stop blaming others for the way they are, and accept responsibility for their present attitudes. This means that if there is any resentment in your heart toward others for some hurt or failure toward you, then you must forgive.

Third, we must ask ourselves if we really want to be healed and delivered. This is what Jesus asked the man who had been ill for thirty-eight years: "Do you want to be made well?" (John 5:6, NKJ). You see, it is possible that past problems serve a purpose for us.

One purpose might be to use them as a crutch so that we can walk with a limp and thus get the sympathy of others. Another purpose could be to use the hurts one has received as an excuse to hurt others.

The fourth thing is to bring whatever is troubling you to God and ask Him to heal it. If you go through the other three steps carefully, this last step will be a very easy one. If nothing happens, then go over the first three steps again, something is being missed. Whenever we do our part, God never fails to do His.

Chapter 14

SHARING GOD

*"For Christ's love compels us, because we are
convinced that one died for all, and therefore
all died."*
(2 Corinthians 5:14, NIV)

We continue meditating on some of the ways we can
sharpen the awareness of God's presence in our lives.
One such way is to ensure that we give out what God
puts in. I call this *the discipline of sharing*. We should
discipline ourselves as definitely to share by word
and deed what we know of God as we do to pray and
read the Scriptures.

Take the initiative

Many do not do this. They are earnest and regular in
their Quiet Times, but they have never disciplined
themselves to share. If an event or a conversation,
bumping against them, jolts it out of them, all well
and good. But this kind of sharing is more by accident
than by choice; a question of whim rather than a
question of will. The natural impulse of a heart in

which God's love and presence dwells is to radiate that love and presence to others.

You might have heard the story of the man who, finding a little dog by the roadside with a broken leg, took it to his house and attended to it until it was well. It began to run around the house and then, one day, it disappeared. The man had grown to love the little dog and felt somewhat disappointed and let down; but the next day there was a scratching at the door. The little dog was back again, but this time there was another little dog with it, and the other little dog was lame! The impulse in that little dog's heart was right. It was the impulse to share what it had received with others. Does God's love and presence abide in you? Good. It will get even deeper and richer as you take the initiative in sharing His love and presence with others.

If it has not occurred to you already, then the point must be made now, that the practice of the presence of God involves discipline. Some of the things I am suggesting in this book need deliberate and concentrated effort. It is much easier to relax and let things happen of their own accord, but, in my experience, it is the disciplined who get the best results.

No freedom without law

There are those who will object and say, "We are made for freedom, all this talk about discipline is foreign to Christianity." But freedom can only come through disciplined obedience. I am free from pressure by the police only as I obey the law; within the framework of the law they represent, I am free.

Someone has put it like this: "I am free to swing my arm, but my freedom ends at the tip of your nose."

There is no such thing as absolute freedom. Freedom, if it means anything at all, must be controlled by law. And it is a law of the kingdom of God that what goes on in the soul must pass through the soul. Intake must result in outflow. I once heard a preacher say: "God is like electricity: He won't come in unless He can get out." Well, God is not quite like that, but I am sure you can see the point he was making. God is not interested in just living *in* us; He is interested in living *through* us. The joyous thing about sharing with others what God has put inside us is that we become all the better for the sharing. As we give, so we receive; and not only do we become better, we become better off. We experience His presence in a more real and wonderful way.

Don't be a hearer only

Over the years, both in letters and in private conversation with fellow Christians, I have been presented with this question: "I have known the presence of God in my life in a real and vital way, but now, for some reason, it seems to have ebbed away. Why is this?" There could be many reasons why this is so, but I have often found that a major cause for this is a failure to share what they know of God with others. If there is no outflow, the inflow automatically stops. It is a law of life that whatever is not used atrophies, or dies. Professor Henry Drummond, in his book *Natural Law in the Spiritual World*, talks about some fish caught in the dark waters of the Mammoth Caves in

Kentucky, USA, in which it was found that although they had eyes, they could not really see. No one quite knows how they got into the caves, but there in the darkness, where no natural light ever penetrated, eyesight became superfluous. "Nature," said Professor Henry Drummond, "adopted the position – what you don't use, you don't need."

Now, of course, we must not push this too far and suggest that if we do not work at sharing God's love and presence with others, we will lose our salvation, because that is not what Scripture teaches. It is a fact, however, that the more we share what we have received, the more we will have to share. Revelation 22:17, "The Spirit and the bride say, 'Come!' And let him who hears say, 'Come!' ..." (NIV) challenged me greatly in my teenage years. When I read it, the Spirit said to me: "You have been a hearer – now say 'Come'." I went out and won my first soul to Christ.

Four steps in sharing

Many people are hesitant to share the love and presence of God with others because they do not know how to go about it. I dislike exceedingly the idea of "selling religion", it smacks of commercialism and makes Christ appear to be a commodity. Nevertheless, there are some things we can learn from those whose task it is to sell commodities.

I have had a lot to do with sales people in my time, and I have noticed that some get a lot of customers, while others get none. The ones who make an impression usually do so because of two basic things. One is that they act as though the thing they are selling is of great importance to them, and, two, they do not push too hard, for they know this might produce an unfavourable reaction. I heard a sales manager give four steps in presenting a commodity: (1) What is it? (2) What will it do for you? (3) Who says so? (4) How can you get it?

I commend these four steps to those of you who find difficulty in sharing with others what God has shared with you. What is it? First, clear away misconceptions, and point out what it is not. It is not being joined to a religion, but being joined to a person – Christ. What will it do for you? You will find forgiveness, freedom, reality, a sense of inner unity and of "coming home". Who says so? Christ does – through His word and through the testimony of multitudes of His followers. How can you get it? By repenting of sin – not just wrong habits and actions, but the basic sin of self-dependency – depending on self rather than on God. I recommend these four questions as a framework for sharing Christ with others. They have worked for me, and for many others. I have a conviction they may also work for you.

Chapter 15

OVERCOMING WITH GOD

*". . . count it all joy when you fall into various
trials, knowing that the testing of your faith
produces patience."*
(James 1:2–3, NKJ)

We now come to the final suggestion I have to offer
on how to sharpen the awareness of God's presence
in your heart, by *willingly and joyfully opening the door
of your life to any trials and tribulations that may knock
upon it.*

I know this statement will be difficult for many to
accept, but let's begin by seeing how firmly rooted it
is in Scripture. I am sure that many will have seen the
J.B. Phillips paraphrase of the text which introduces
this chapter, but in case you have not, or you have
forgotten it, this is what it says:

"When all kinds of trials and temptations crowd
into your lives, my brothers, don't resent them as
intruders, but welcome them as friends! Realise
that they come to test your faith and to produce in
you the quality of endurance."

Can you see the tremendous truth that is contained in these words? They are saying that when we open the door of our lives to trials and temptations, they serve, not to demean us, but to develop us. Now what is our natural response when something knocks at the door of our lives, and upon opening it, we find standing there a particularly unwelcome trial or temptation? Is it not quickly to slam the door in its face? Well, Scripture is telling us that there is a better response – open wide the door and welcome it in as you would a long-lost friend. How strange. Why does Scripture tell us to do this? Here is the answer – because trials and temptations will, if we respond to them correctly, cause us to rely less on our own strength and more on the strength of Christ. The difficulties become the doors through which His presence flows more power-fully into our lives.

The island of revelation

Look at this passage, Revelation 1:9–10: "I, John, your brother and companion in the suffering and kingdom and patient endurance that are ours in Jesus, was on the island of Patmos because of the word of God and the testimony of Jesus. On the Lord's Day I was in the Spirit, and I heard behind me a loud voice like a trumpet . . ." (NIV), for example. The apostle John says: "I . . . was on the isle called Patmos, (banished) on account of my witnessing to the Word of God . . ." (Amp. Bible). He experienced one of the greatest trials that anyone could be called upon to endure, banishment and isolation. He was bereft of the presence of his Christian friends and companions, but was he bereft of the presence of God? Listen to what he says: "I was in the Spirit – rapt in His power – on the Lord's day, and I heard behind me a great voice . . ." (v10: Amp. Bible). Shut off from men, he was open to God.

Am I talking to someone right now who is experiencing a trial of banishment and isolation? I don't mean that you have been carried off to some lonely island in the middle of the ocean, but put in some situation where you feel bereft of Christian fellowship. Then, take heart, for the island of isolation can be an island of revelation. God will not fail you. He will, if you do your part by accepting the position in which you find yourself, make His presence so vital and real to you, that you will come out from this episode of your life realising the truth of Paul's great words in Romans 8: "Neither death nor life, nor angels nor principalities nor powers, nor things present nor things to come . . . shall be able to separate us from the love of God which is in Christ Jesus our Lord" (vv. 38–39: NKJ). When you are shut off from the presence of others, it will serve only to enable you to feel the presence of Christ more keenly.

Be willing

It is probably safe to say that one of the reasons why we may not experience a rich and satisfying sense of God's presence in our lives is due to our unwillingness to face life's trials and temptations. You see, if we are afraid to face a trial or a temptation, then we will never experience the deep power of Christ's compensating presence in the midst of those trials and temptations. If only we could grasp the truth that, in Christ, nothing can work successfully against us. It can only work for us. When a trial comes our way, it means that we will experience even more deeply and keenly the sustaining power and presence of our Lord Jesus Christ. Can you see now why the Scripture encourages us to welcome trials and temptations? They serve a divine purpose by opening us up to knowing Christ's presence in a deeper and more wonderful way.

I met a man once who told me that when his doctor informed him that he had terminal cancer, he went into a state of shock for a few days. When he came out of it, he said to himself: "All right, if this is so, then by life and death – I want to glorify the Lord." He set about re-establishing his priorities and focused on how he could best minister to people during his last few months on this earth. When I asked him what was the one thing above all else that he could be thankful for, he replied with tears in his eyes: "The presence of Christ, the presence of Christ."

A guide and an inexperienced climber had to spend all night in the Pyrenees; they couldn't make it back. Toward dawn, there was a tempestuous wind that twisted trees and started rocks rolling down the mountainsides; and, as you can imagine, the inexperienced climber was terrified. The guide reassured him: "Don't worry, this is the way the dawn usually comes high up here in the Pyrenees." And sometimes our dawn comes through the storms of trials and temptations, the dawn of a deeper encounter with God.

John Wilhelm Rowntree, a Christian writer on the

West Coast of America, tells how, when he left a doctor's office after being told that his advancing blindness could not be halted, he stood by some railings for a few minutes to collect himself. "Suddenly," he says, "I felt the love of God wrap me about as though an invisible presence enfolded me, and a joy filled me such as I had never known before."

Believe me, that presence will manifest itself when most needed. Luke 22:39–53 shows us how Christ went into the Garden of Gethsemane and endured such agony that it says an angel was sent to strengthen Him: "And there appeared to Him an angel from heaven, strengthening Him in spirit" (v.43: Amp. Bible). In the hour of His greatest need, He experienced the greatest strengthening. You may be called on to face a "Gethsemane" experience. If so, then remember, you can come out of it, as did Jesus, with a deeper sense of God's strengthening and enabling presence than you ever knew before.

Chapter 16

PRACTICE MAKES PERFECT

". . . you will fill me with joy in your presence,
with eternal pleasures at your right hand."
(Psalm 16:11, NIV)

We come finally to ask ourselves: what are some of the benefits that flow from an increased awareness of God's presence in our lives?

The first benefit is that it makes us stronger in faith. The more we realise that, by a simple act of memory, we can sharpen the awareness of God's presence in our hearts, the more easily we will be able to put our faith into operation in the bigger and wider issues of our lives.

The second benefit is that it makes us stronger in hope. "Hope," says E.M. Blaiklock, "grows in proportion to our knowledge, and according as our faith penetrates through this holy exercise (reminding ourselves that God's presence is constantly with us) into the secrets of the Divine . . . our hope grows and strengthens itself, and the grandeur of this good which it seeks to enjoy, and in some manner tastes, reassures and sustains it."

A third benefit is that it makes us stronger in love. The more we gaze upon God, the more we will love Him, and, of course, the converse is also true – the more we love Him, the more we will gaze upon Him. The more we practise His presence, the more perfectly we will feel His presence.

So remember, my friend, you are not alone. At the time of seeming aloneness, He is closer to you than you realise, watching every move you make on the chessboard of life. But do not take His presence for granted, practise it. He has said He will never leave you nor forsake you, but you must constantly remind yourself of that fact. Like all things in life, practice makes perfect. Go out now, then, and from this time forward, determine to practise the presence of God.

PRAYER
O God, help me to put into practice the things You have taught me. Help me to beautify the hours as they come and go by experiencing Your presence in my life in a way I have never known before. In Jesus' Name I ask it. Amen.

REVIVAL
Times of Refreshing
Selwyn Hughes

Without doubt one of the greatest themes of Scripture is "heaven-sent" revival.

"Heaven sent" because real revival is not something that springs up or out of the normal activities of the Christian Church but something that comes down from above.

In *Revival – Times of Refreshing* Selwyn Hughes explores what revival is – and isn't. He looks at past revivals to examine how we, and the Church as a whole, are prepared by God for revival so that we may know how to respond.

Has God got something bigger in His heart for us than we are at present seeing? Yes, says Selwyn Hughes, God is able to do greater and yet more wondrous things. He has reserves of power which we, the Church of this generation, have not fully experienced. Our task is to lay hold on His highest willingness.

UNDERSTANDING GUIDANCE
Selwyn Hughes

In *Understanding Guidance*, Selwyn Hughes discusses the problems and perplexities we all face as Christians who are trying to lead a God-guided life.

Finding God's will, he shows, is not about following formulas; it is maintaining a loving relationship with the One who wants to guide us. Upon this foundation, he takes a careful look at the ways God guides and the freedom He gives for us to choose.

A final section offers a practical step by step guide to knowing God's will.